Dear Parent:
Your child's love of reading starts here!

Every child learns to read in a different way and at his or her own speed. Some go back and forth between reading levels and read favorite books again and again. Others read through each level in order. You can help your young reader improve and become more confident by encouraging his or her own interests and abilities. From books your child reads with you to the first books he or she reads alone, there are I Can Read Books for every stage of reading:

SHARED READING
Basic language, word repetition, and whimsical illustrations, ideal for sharing with your emergent reader

BEGINNING READING
Short sentences, familiar words, and simple concepts for children eager to read on their own

READING WITH HELP
Engaging stories, longer sentences, and language play for developing readers

READING ALONE
Complex plots, challenging vocabulary, and high-interest topics for the independent reader

ADVANCED READING
Short paragraphs, chapters, and exciting themes for the perfect bridge to chapter books

I Can Read Books have introduced children to the joy of reading since 1957. Featuring award-winning authors and illustrators and a fabulous cast of beloved characters, I Can Read Books set the standard for beginning readers.

A lifetime of discovery begins with the magical words **"I Can Read!"**

Visit www.icanread.com for information
on enriching your child's reading experience.

Pinkalicious

at the Fair

To Emerson

—V.K.

The author gratefully acknowledges
the artistic and editorial contributions of
Dan Griffo and Jacqueline Resnick.

I Can Read Book® is a trademark of HarperCollins Publishers.

Pinkalicious at the Fair
Copyright © 2018 by Victoria Kann

PINKALICIOUS and all related logos and characters are trademarks of Victoria Kann. Used with permission.

Based on the HarperCollins book *Pinkalicious* written by
Victoria Kann and Elizabeth Kann, illustrated by Victoria Kann
All rights reserved. Manufactured in China.
No part of this book may be used or reproduced in any manner whatsoever without
written permission except in the case of brief quotations embodied in critical articles and reviews.
For information address HarperCollins Children's Books, a division of HarperCollins Publishers,
195 Broadway, New York, NY 10007.
www.icanread.com

Library of Congress Control Number: 2017942885

ISBN 978-0-06-256694-2 (trade bdg.) — ISBN 978-0-06-256691-1 (pbk.)

17 18 19 20 21 SCP 10 9 8 7 6 5 4 3 2 1
❖
First Edition

I Can Read!

BEGINNING READING 1

Pinkalicious

at the Fair

by Victoria Kann

HARPER

An Imprint of HarperCollinsPublishers

Cotton candy!

A pet show!

Rides!

I didn't know what to do first.

Molly and I were at the

Pinkville Fair with Mommy.

"Let's start at the

merry-go-round!" Mommy said.

8

Molly rode an elephant.

I chose a beautiful white horse.

Mommy waved when we passed.

"Everything's spinning,"

I said, giggling.

My horse went up and down.

It reminded me of my unicorn,

Goldilicious.

"It's just like riding

Goldie!" I said.

"Too bad she stayed home."

"I wish I had a unicorn,"
said Molly.
"You can always
play with mine," I said.
"That's what friends are for."

We got cotton candy next.

It's a fair tradition!

"It's too bad Goldie isn't here,"
I said.

"She loves pink treats."

Molly and I played every game!

My favorite was

the Unicorn Ring Toss.

"I got one!" I said.

"Me too!" said Molly.

We each got to pick a prize.

We chose friendship charms.

Each charm was half a heart.

We pressed the halves together

to make a whole heart.

"I'm glad you're my friend,
Pinkalicious," Molly said.
"I'm glad, too," I said.

We wore our new charms
to the pet show.

There were so many animals!

I held a duck.

Molly petted a piglet!

"The blue ribbon goes to . . . Fluffy!"

said a judge.

A girl walked up with her lamb.
The judge put a big ribbon
on its collar.

Seeing all the animals made me sad.

My unicorn was the best of all!

"I wish Goldie was here," I said.

"She would win a prize."

"She deserves a ribbon," said Molly.

I missed my unicorn.

Suddenly I felt a soft nudge.

I turned around.

It was Goldie!

I threw my arms around her
and hugged her tight.
That's when I saw something.
Goldie wasn't alone!

"Look!" Molly said.

"Goldie is here!"

"It looks like she

has a friend!" I said.

Goldie nuzzled me.

So did her friend.

"How fantastic!" said Molly.

"No," I said with a smile.

"How PINKATASTIC!"

"I'm glad you have a best
friend, too,"
I told Goldie.

That gave me an idea.

I took off my charm.

So did Molly.

We gave them to the unicorns.

"The next prize goes to . . .

Goldie and her pal!" I announced.

"For being the best unicorns—

and the best friends!"

Friends forever!